#write

C000112977

"Writing my memoir wi
me feel a part of a greater story of standing in truth
upon this earth. I am eternally grateful for Betsy and
her loyalty to truth and healing." - Maggie Marie

"I love how Betsy swallowed the sun and now it beams
out from everything she does—pleasure activism,
writing, loving her kids, loving her community,
and most of all loving herself. I love the way Betsy
has transformed what has hurt her into what heals
her, and how she's danced forward into the eternal
What's Next." - Jennifer Gandin Le

"I have such gratitude for how gentle and encouraging
Betsy was with my writing and how that feeling of
safety allowed me to dig deeper." - Elisabeth

"Betsy's intuitive writing prompts have uncovered the story within and taken me down writing pathways I could've never imagined." - Melanie

"Betsy's writing prompts made me pull out threads from my life tapestry. I twisted them to re-examine individual heartbeats and to revisit the sights, sounds, smells, and most importantly the feelings. I realized fifteen minutes every day was just enough to tease this process. I'm inspired to return to each of the prompts and pull more threads!" - Christine

"Women like Betsy who are so supportive and loving to other women are a rare breed in my experience." - Victoria

"There is no better person than Betsy to help you start telling your stories." - Susie

Beautiful Infinity Books

United States

www.betsybmurphy.com

A Daily Writing Practice
for Anyone with a Story to Tell

Write On.

Betsy B. Murphy

Beautiful Infinity Books
United States

*Writing should liberate you
instead of making you feel stuck.*

Table of Contents

For the Unexpressed Stories of All Hearts

This book is dedicated to the unexpressed stories of all hearts and especially to a friend I met only through her words, Virginia Fox.

"I'm trying to understand why I am hurting. I know your books will help me," she wrote. And so began a correspondence that lasted less than a year but seemed like a lifetime.

I met Virginia Fox first through Instagram and then on Facebook. Her posts and her messages always justified slowing down and savoring.

She started by joining in my 40 Days of Writing Prompts in 2019. Every one of her stories took me into a world that was unfamiliar to me, but my heart lifted with each sentence. I always wanted to read on to find out what happened next. This extraordinary woman lived a life of stories.

While I was a teenager in the 1970s, Virginia's photos from that time show an elegant, adventurous woman who was probably ten to fifteen years older than me. She was who I dreamed of being! Virginia was an expert on art and architecture. She was passionate about Formula One racing. She spoke fluent Italian and French. She loved dancing and music and often sent me songs to consider for Qoya classes. She had never taken one but imagined it was like when she would "blast the music at night and dance like a whirling dervish under the olive trees on a vineyard in South Africa... there always seemed to be a moon above. I was at peace, dancing heaven on earth... Was that my version of Qoya?" she asked in one of her notes to me.

I never met Virginia in person, but I got to know her through her stories. She lived a life that at times included private planes and yachts. She also experienced great love and great loss. I witnessed her being a cheerleader to others, trying to be of service even as she shared with me that her own recent health issues left her in constant pain. And like so many of us, sometimes writing about the painful moments of her life didn't feel good, but once she did, she discovered medicine in her own words.

Virginia had a gift for seducing the senses with her storytelling. I was always reminding her that she should write a book. During the summer of 2019, I realized I hadn't heard from her in a while, so I looked her up. I saw that she was still posting music and dances and racing moments that moved her. Her last message to me was a reminder to savor the smell of lavender growing wild. I started to write her back and then got busy and decided to write another day. A few weeks later, I discovered she had passed from an illness that quickly shut down her organs.

I will leave you with the words she sent to me by Rumi. This was the last thing she wrote to me.

All the precious words
you and I have exchanged
have found their way
into the heart of the universe
One day they'll pour on us
like whispering rain
helping us arise
from our roots again.

Thank you, Virginia, for trusting me with your stories.

To anyone reading this book, may the stories revealed to you during the daily writing prompts nourish your roots and your spirt and may you always remember that your story connects to the heartbeat of the universe where every voice matters.

Ready, Set, Write On

D ear Storyteller,

If this book has found its way to you, take it as a sign that you should write your story.

This book has 365 days of writing prompts. If you commit to doing the prompts daily for fifteen minutes, at the end of a year you'll have over 200,000 words. If you are thinking about writing a book, that's about three books worth of material. If you are wanting to write a TED-style talk, that's over 300 ideas for a talk. If you need to write newsletters, that's a year of inspiration for newsletters.

This book also includes bonus writing and publishing information on what helped me as I was writing my first book (*Autobiography of an Orgasm,* released in 2014). The success of that book, which I self-published, led me to start my own publishing platform, *Beautiful Infinity Books.* I also believe in traditional publishing, but just because something has been done one way for years doesn't mean that is the only way.

If you are considering writing a book and need to find your writer's voice, start with the daily prompts in *Write On.* I also recommend reading Mark Shaw's *How to Become a Published Author: Idea to Publication.* Shaw's book is packed full of valuable information, so you'll become knowledgeable about the writing process and the publishing industry.

For the past ten years, I've sat in circles with storytellers from all over the world, and most have one thing in common. They say, "I'm not a writer. I don't even know where to begin."

My answer is to not start at the beginning. Let's allow your intuition and imagination to guide you. And if you don't want to proclaim yourself a writer, then let's call you a storyteller. We all have a good story in us. These prompts will help you tell one good story. And if you can tell one good story, you can write one good book or give one good TED talk or write one good newsletter.

These writing prompts are designed for fifteen-minute writing sessions. Everyone who has done them is always surprised by the stories that are revealed. I hear comments like, "I haven't thought about that for years" or "I've never told anyone this" or "It feels good to remember."

The writing prompts may bring up stories you have never shared or never wanted to share. Allow the writing to guide you through the story. It's come up again for a reason. Writing continues to help me make sense of the parts of my life that I thought belonged only in therapy!

My hope is that you will read each prompt when you have fifteen minutes to devote to writing. If you are not ready to write, maybe close the book and open it later. Consider doing the first forty prompts in order. After that, you can use them like an oracle—pick a number and open to that page, perhaps calling in the perfect inspiration for that moment.

While the writing suggestions are designed for personal history storytelling, you can also call on your imagination and write fiction. You can use each prompt more than once. I've found that every time I begin writing inspired by a particular prompt, the story is always different, even if I've written on the subject before. If you are already working on a book, the prompts will allow you to see your story from a different perspective.

This exercise is a way to witness life—from extraordinary situations that feel like magic to the simple moments that feel mundane—writing about your life brings meaning to it all while building your creative muscle.

You can write on your laptop or put pen to paper. It's preferable to write for only fifteen minutes on the prompt. If you like what's coming through on the page, you can go back to it later and add more or revise.

Once you read the prompt, commit to writing for fifteen minutes. If the prompt doesn't inspire anything, then that is your first sentence; just keep writing it until another sentence comes to you. For example, if the prompt is **Tell me what you wanted to be when you were eight years old** and nothing comes up for you, your story may start with *I don't remember what I wanted to be when I was eight.* And then continue from there. Don't walk away and try again later. The idea is to access what is coming through in the present moment. Even if you're writing the same sentence over and over, eventually your intuition will take you beyond that sentence and then beyond the next sentence. The story may end up having nothing to do with beingeight.

You can do the writing prompts on your own or invite a friend or family member to do them with you and commit to reading your stories to each other so your words can be witnessed. I suggest you do this without feedback as a way to practice speaking and listening from your heart or soul space. When we deeply listen to each other without needing to respond, we allow the sacred to be present.

Writing is a way to bring the sacred into a written and spoken expression. Through writing prompts, we look deeper into what is guiding our spirits, learn how to tell the hard stories, use humor to relate to the reader, and discover where our own stories connect to a bigger story.

What are the unexpressed stories of your life? Let's take the time to write them. They may be just what someone else needs to read.

Ready? Write On.

Love from Betsy

www.betsybmurphy.com

1

The Japanese have an art form called kintsugi, which uses a gold dust to repair broken pottery. The gold design of the crack becomes part of its beauty and history.

Tell about something that broke or cracked.

2

In 2018, I decided to take my mother's maiden name, Murphy, as my last name. I've been thinking about doing it for a while. While I'm proud of my father and proud to be a Blankenbaker, I've always felt like more of a Murphy.

What is the story of your name?

(It could be first, last, both or wherever the prompt takes you.)

3

This prompt is in two parts so we can work with the five senses. The senses are a way to make your stories vivid, so you are showing the story instead of just telling it. Instead of writing, *It started to rain*, write about the smell of the rain on the grass, the coolness of the raindrops on your skin or the color of the sky and sound of the raindrops on the window.

Imagine you are ten years old again. Spend a minute or so making a list for each sense.

What is the taste of being ten?

What is the smell of being ten?

What do you see around you?

What do you hear?

What does ten feel like? (touch...)

What did you want to be when you were ten years old?

Try to include some of the senses you listed.

4

My son Willie is a comedian based in Chicago. Often when we speak, it looks like he is typing something. "I'm not ignoring you," he says. "I just want to remember what you said so I can work it into my show." As the brilliant Nora Ephron said, "Everything is copy."

As I was writing my first book, there was a concern about writing about family or the men from my past relationships. Before the book was released, I sent chapters involving those men to tell them I was sharing my story and that I would change their names in the book. One of the men gave me his blessing to share our story and use his name, another man threatened to sue me.

When I met Elizabeth Gilbert (*Eat, Pray, Love*) at a book event, she reminded me "If they wanted you to write better things about them, they should have treated you better." The point is when you are writing about family you must remember you are not telling the family story; you are telling YOUR story about your place in the family.

Tell about something your mother or father said to you.

5

Some of my favorite stories to read are true stories of the unseen, unexplainable, and unbelievable events that occur in our lives. These events don't make sense in an ordinary, organized world but when I read about them, I can feel the authenticity of the storyteller's words in the pulse of my cells. Some of these mystical events may occur in our daily lives, some occur in our dreams.

If I'm paying attention, I see mystical signs and synchronicities in my daily life. I'm sure you do too.

Tell about a mystical or magical moment in your life - an event that didn't make sense, but you know to be true.

Begin your story with the line, *This doesn't make sense, but it happened.*

6

The *Wizard of Oz* begins with a tornado. Weather can be used in storytelling as a metaphor for what is occurring in our lives. You can also use a change in the weather as inspiration for your story.

Tell about a time it began to rain harder, or the earth shook, or the waves pulled you under.

7

The prompts are meant to inspire personal storytelling. The stories I connect most with aren't just when writers tell the truth, but when they do so in a daring way. One person who does well at writing on the edge is my friend Kaci Florez. Kaci writes daringly about her husband's sudden death in 2015. At the age of 29, she became a widow.

Here is an excerpt from her story:

I don't remember much else of what she said but "He's gone."

Pacing, I began to ask questions for more information. She didn't have more information. I had been awaiting his call that day. I realized that call would never come.

I remember screaming and crawling on the floor. I remember hitting the couch cushions. I remember what it felt like to be unable to comprehend the fullness of a piece of information I had been given.

My husband was gone.

That thought was too big to take in all at one time. His call would never come. I would not get to talk to him again. I would not get to hear from him what was going on.

I had so many questions that only he could answer. Only he could tell me the whole story. And I would never get to hear the story from him.

In the blur of shock and confusion during those first few moments of receiving the news, my next thought was "I never get to have sex with him again." The deepest and most intimate physical act. I'm not even sure if I had hung up with his sister yet when I looked at our bed and realized that we would never express our love through our physical bodies or give one another pleasure again.

Write On.

I remember being a little surprised that this thought came to me so early on. Was I being shallow? Did it reveal a lack of depth to our relationship that I was lamenting our physical intimacy so early on? When I heard other people talk about losing their spouses, I don't remember hearing sex being missed so quickly. Were they just holding something back? Was I just not hearing them? Was society not ready to hear them? Was this inappropriate to talk about? This was a moment that I felt the invisible expectations of societal norms and realized I could no longer pretend to fit within them.

Excerpt from Chapter 1 of *Autobiographies of Our Orgasms, Vol. 3*

Prompt #3: **Tell about the last time.** (This prompt isn't necessarily meant to be about sex...let your intuition guide the writing.)

8

There is a gang of hummingbirds that lives my backyard. They intuitively know to go to the flowers with the sweetest nectar, the flowers that bring them joy. And they know which flowers to avoid. There comes a moment in life, maybe more than once, when we choose the flower with the sweetest nectar. We trust our intuition.

Tell about a time you trusted your intuition.

9

I've never been good at fixing things. When my last car needed new tires, alignment, and some other issues fixed, I got rid of the car. (And have never replaced it.) Like my car, so many of us just walk away instead of trying to fix something. Or we discard the old and buy it new. Sometimes it's a car; sometimes it's a relationship.

Tell about something you tried to fix.

10

If there was a language of the heart, Mary Oliver spoke that language through her poems. She managed to write the things I needed to hear and one of them was to be astonished by my life. For so many years, I'd only carried shame about the secrets, about the mistakes, about the disappointments. And then Oliver's poetry asked me to pay attention and be astonished. She asked me to simply witness my life instead of judging it.

Tell how your life astonishes you.

11

One empowering thing about writing memoir - or our personal history - is the ability to go back and rewrite moments that may have been out of our control. For me, this is when the writing moves from being authentic to also being medicine.

One of the writing prompts that changed my life was writing my birth story. When I was born my three siblings had the children pox, so I went home to my godparent's house for the first weeks of my life instead of being with my family. For years, I could never understand how my parents could 'give' me away! In my early 50s, I was invited to write my birth story for a book called, *Birth Your Story* by Jaime Fleres, and writing the story made me see my birth in a completely different way.

My godparents lost a baby eight years before I was born - a girl who was stillborn. My godmother was so upset that she refused to hold her dead daughter. Eight years later, when I was placed into my godmother Betty's arms, my god sister Cathy told me that is when the healing started for my godparents. Suddenly, I loved my mother enormously for offering her baby to someone who needed to heal.

During a writing retreat when I asked the writers to share their birth stories, one woman who had the experience of a traumatic birth decided to rewrite her birth story using her imagination to write the birth story she always wanted for herself. Sometimes choosing to write our stories with new details is a powerful way to heal.

Write your birth story. You can either write the story of your own birth or if you are a parent, you can write the story of the birth of one of your children.

12

About ten years ago, I was visiting my home state of Indiana and was at a restaurant getting carryout. I ran into a man that I knew from my former life when I was mostly known as "the wife of ..." When I was married, this man and his wife had been acquaintances. He didn't know me too well, and he knew even less about me since I'd been divorced and moved to Miami. I'd released several documentary films to great reviews but low box office sales. I was co-raising four children with my former husband. I was living a good life in the midst of loss and divorce.

As I waited for my order, this man moved down the bar towards me. I couldn't avoid him. My gut was churning before he even reached me, and it wasn't from hunger. This man immediately started firing questions at me, "Where are you living now? (Your ex) has another child? I heard you made a movie. How much did the movie make? Who is your boyfriend? Are you getting married again?"

The questions came fast — he wasn't listening to my answers before he asked the next one. I shared a few details, but not too much because I could tell he was only interested in the parts of the story that felt more like gossip. When he heard that my film didn't make money and that I wasn't dating anyone he said to me, "I guess life hasn't worked out for you, has it?"

One way to make peace with statements projected towards you is to write about them. If we don't tell it, parts of us are erased or get lost in other people's stories about us.

The prompt is:

This is what I forgot to tell you.

or

This is what you don't know about me.

13

I often hear from people that they don't know what to write about. Start with the themes and patterns in your life. Make a list. Those themes will come up over and over again in your writing.

My first book was about healing my body. The next book was about living without a home in the world and realizing that I needed to remember and care for my first home, my body. I also write about family and how culture views the mother, the matriarch, and her body. See the pattern?

As you pay attention to what themes come up again and again in your life, also pay attention to the stuck places in your body, where do you feel tight?

Where you feel stuck is where the story is.

Take a minute to make a list of patterns in your life.

Tell about where you feel tight or stuck in your body.

(And maybe how it relates to a part of life where you've been stuck, reserved, limited.)

14

From the age of six until 45, I had frequent sore throats and strep throats and laryngitis. When I got divorced, I literally lost my voice for three weeks but really, I lost it years earlier when I didn't speak up around abuse. When you are six and ten, you don't even have the words. Even into my forties, I was still staying quiet around abuse to my physical and emotional health. And then I started writing my story and speaking my story and guess what? I haven't had a sore throat in ten years. I used to be sick at least once a month with flu-like symptoms. I'm never sick. So, yes, speaking your truth has consequences, you may start to be healthier.

The truth is ... This may come out as a list or a story. Just allow the thoughts to flow.

15

The writer and actress Ann Randolph performed her show *Squeeze Box* on Broadway. It was produced by Mel Brooks and Anne Bancroft. Several years ago, I took one of Ann's writing workshops in California and then committed to taking one of her stage workshops in Kauai. I had never considered turning my book into a solo show, but then I witnessed how Ann turned her tragedies into triumph - and made it entertaining. I was also curious about the connection between speaking up as medicine. Can telling our stories out loud, even to just one person, be a component of healing?

One of the writing exercises Ann turned me onto is called "Yay/Boo" and I always do it with writers on my retreats. The idea is to discover the turning points of your story by writing sentences that either gets a "Yay" (something good happens to you) or a "Boo" (something challenging/disappointing happens to you). It's depressing to read stories where something bad happens and then another bad thing happens and then another bad thing happens. And we also don't want to read about only good things happening to the lead character in the story. We need a reason to cheer you on.

Tell about a big win (Yay).

Tell about a big disappointment (Boo).

Tell about a big recovery (Yay) in your life.

16

When I write in a journal, the story may just be about what happened to me (*Dear Journal, This is what happened to me. Why me?!!*). As I begin to switch from stream of conscious writing into crafting a story with structure, I move into: *This is what happened to me - and it happened over and over again until the moment when I finally changed.*

It's the concept of: "I used to be... but now I'm..."

I used to stay quiet, but now I speak up about things that matter to me. I used to disconnect from my body when I didn't feel safe, but now I stay present and allow myself to feel everything.

Spend two minutes making a list of: I used to... but now I'm...

Write On.

Now choose one and write about it for 15 minutes. It may come out as a full story; it may come out as journal writing...it doesn't matter!

I used to care about turning the writing prompts into a story, but now I just follow my intuition for 15 minutes and write whatever wants to show up.

17

If you haven't seen it, make sure you watch the Fred Rogers documentary, *Won't You Be My Neighbor?* There is a point in the film when the people interviewed are asked to think about the helpers in their lives - the people who showed up during difficult times. The movie audio goes silent for a minute, but you can still see and feel the onscreen emotions even though no one is speaking.

If I think about the helpers in my life, it's not always the best friends or loved ones. It's also the random kindness that can show up from a stranger.

Tell about the helpers in your life.

18

On June 8, 2018, my daughter Lucy called me. I could tell she was upset. I was in an airport lounge waiting for a flight wondering if it was bad news about family. Through her tears she said, "Anthony Bourdain died." Lucy loves cooking and feeding people - and she loved Anthony Bourdain. I think Bourdain appealed to so many because he used food as a place to connect with people. His show wasn't just about food. His meals created stories. His stories were about love of food and of people.

Tell about something you made or Tell something someone made for you.

19

By now, maybe you have experienced one story you've written during the writing prompts that felt like medicine to write. Just like exercising for even 15 minutes a day, writing is healing. And writing helps you remember those untold stories that want to be witnessed.

Use the prompt: **I remember...**

Write for 15 minutes. Let the prompt take you wherever your imagination or curiosity guides you.

20

Growing up in the Midwest of the U.S., I always knew how much of my summer vacation was left based on the height of the corn. "Knee high by the fourth of July," is what we were told. When the corn reached my knees, there was still half of the summer left, plenty of time for more swimming, more reading, more sleepovers, and more adventures.

During the summer, every Sunday we would drive to my grandparents' farm to visit and pick whatever vegetables were ready. The corn was always the last to harvest. August when we could finally pick the corn. It was worth the wait.

You could find corn anytime during the year, but we knew to only eat it during the late summer harvest when the corn was ripe and sweet and meant to be consumed on a warm summer night with fireflies lighting the garden. The way I learned to butter corn was by sticking the whole cob on a stick of butter and rolling the cob until all sides were dewy and dripping with butter. On the farm in August and early September, there was always a dish that was only meant for buttering your corn. If you wanted to butter toast, that was a different dish.

For the prompt, choose a food that you only eat in the summer. Now take a minute and describe that food (or what is happening around you when you eat it) using your senses:

Taste:

Sight:

Smell:

Touch:

Hear:

Tell a story about a summer food (or meal).

Try and incorporate some of your senses in describing the experience of enjoying that food.

21

I've been thinking about love and how it shows up in my life - both my external and internal experiences of love. It was an orchid that taught me the impact of not loving myself.

Here's an excerpt from *Autobiography of an Orgasm*:

It would have been easier to throw the orchid away, but instead I took time to remove the dead leaves and stem. I gently watered all the roots, paying attention to the flow of water. Not too much – I didn't want to cause more damage. I put the hydrated plant back into the pot. There was no sign of green. It seemed hopeless, but I knew there was life beneath the dirt.

It was almost bedtime, so I carried the pot to my bedside table. I got ready for bed, and for some reason as I turned off the light on my bedside table, I looked at the pot filled with dirt and said, "I love you." I fell asleep thinking I might be going a little nuts talking to a pot full of dirt and hoping my words might have some impact on its future. Maybe I should have just thrown it away.

The next morning as I woke up, I saw the pot a few feet from my head. I said, "Good morning" and then "I love you" as I moved the pot to the window and opened the shades to let in the sunrise. When I wrote during the day, I moved the pot to my writing table. At night, I put it back on my bedside table. I don't know why, but I continued this pattern daily, making sure to say, "I love you" to the orchid every day. Surely, I thought, I must be crazy.

After a month, a pale green stem pushed through the dirt. It continued to grow, as if remembering who it was before it nearly died. Three months later, some buds appeared on the stem. Over the next few weeks, the buds grew bigger and more numerous. The plant had come back to life. And I did too.

Tell about something you've learned from nature.

22

In the midst of challenging moments, I like to write in the direction I want my life to go. With this prompt, we are going to give ourselves permission to explore our future.

It's five years from now, write a story beginning with:

Just when I thought things couldn't get any better, this happened...

23

Any writing teacher will tell you over and over again: "Show, don't tell, the story."

Notice the different between *Telling* how I met Jean:

Jean was a waiter at a popular French restaurant. At the end of dinner, he wrote his number down on the check. I wasn't sure if I would call him.

And *Showing* how I met Jean:

The first thing he said to me made my backbone tingle.

"Bonsoir, my name is Jean. Can I get you something to drink?"

Why did it feel like hummingbirds were fluttering up my spine?

"I'll have a red wine," I said. My mouth was suddenly dry, but it was more than thirst. His energy was drawing me towards him, even as I sat perfectly still.

Which one would you want to continue reading? It's a choice how we tell our stories so even as we do these prompts, keep remembering to show the story, like a scene from a movie. Your choice of words will entice the reader to keep reading so they can find out what happens next.

The prompt is about the first time you met someone.

Begin your story with: ***The first thing I noticed was ...***

24

In 1999, I interviewed writers John Gregory Dunne and Joan Didion at their apartment in NYC for the first film I ever made, *New York in the Fifties*, based on the book by Dan Wakefield. For the doc, I interviewed Robert Redford (serious), Gay Talese (fun), Nan Talese (intelligent), Bruce Jay Friedman (charming), and close to twenty other writers, poets, painters, and musicians who came of age in New York in the 1950s.

During the interview with John and Joan, John was kind and Joan was formidable. I was relaxed with everyone else, but Joan intimidated me. It was challenging to find a place to connect with her - she lets you into her world through her writing but not when you are sitting with her (and I recognize this quality in myself). I would have been happy to just sit next to Joan as we were both silent.

A few years after the interview, my best friend Sheri died of ovarian cancer. I was sleeping next to her in hospice when she died. It was the same year that Joan lost her husband and her daughter and Joan wrote a book about her grief called, *The Year of Magical Thinking.* That book helped me through my own grief and it also showed me how to write with curiosity. As a writer, I could tell the story and figure out the meaning of things along the way.

My favorite line from that book is when Joan writes that the best gift John ever gave to her is not a physical gift; it is something he said to her.

Tell about a meaningful gift you received.

25

My grandfather was a farmer and a beekeeper and when he would open the hives, it was pure madness. The bees were not orderly, they were flying in all directions. But they intuitively knew to create the hive into hexagons and the six-sided shapes fit together, like chapters of a good book. That's what it's like to write about life. Your life story may get messy in parts but writing helps give it order and meaning. Writing the stories turns them into honey.

One of my favorite reflections of my writing is from Jennifer Gandin Le: «*I love how Betsy swallowed the sun and now it beams out from everything she does— pleasure activism, writing, loving her kids, loving her community, and most of all loving herself. I love the way Betsy has transformed what has hurt her into what heals her, and how she's danced forward into the eternal What's Next."*

Two great prompts to spark stories are: **The first time** or **The last time.**

For today, the writing prompt is meant to inspire what will happen the next time. What happens the next time you swallow the sun, speak up, make a mistake, fall in love, go home, try something new, take a road trip, tell the truth, or go make honey. What's next?

Tell a story about the next time.

26

One of the things I love about writing memoir is remembering who I am and also remembering who I used to be. Writing allows me to witness my younger self, my present self, and write in the direction of my future self.

In the exploration of self, I've done many spiritual retreats and pilgrimages to sacred sights. It's odd because as I traveled further away from home, I felt more like myself. It had nothing to do with the sacred site. For me, it's the same with writing. The more I write, the more I remember who I am and the more I feel like myself.

Tell about a sacred site that feels like home.

27

Summers remind me of family road trips to Canada. It was the 1970s and my parents had a 32-foot motorhome that we used for family vacations. With Mom, Dad and five kids, air travel was too expensive for us so twice a year - for spring break and for summer vacation - we would load up the motorhome.

The motorhome was about 300 square feet. We learned to not take up too much space. Even now I can travel for three weeks with carry-on luggage only because in the motorhome, I had a cubbyhole the size of an extra small suitcase.

Tell about what is in your suitcase or **Tell about what you left behind.**

28

There is a fascinating Radiolab podcast about Albert Einstein and what happened to his brain after he died. The episode is mostly about the story around his stolen brain but there is also mention of his wife, Mileva Maric, whom he met at university in Zurich where they were both studying math and science. They got married and began having kids. Maric dropped out of the program to become a mom and wife. But there are letters between them where Einstein writes about, "...our work on the relative motion..." Was a woman a part of developing the Theory of Relativity with Einstein and never credited?!

This writing prompt is centered around something a woman said to you. Take two minutes and make a list of things you've been told by a woman. The quotes may come from the same woman (a friend, sister, mother or grandmother) or each quote may be from different women. It may be a quote from someone you don't know but are inspired by her words. After you make your list, choose one quote from that list to begin your story.

Take two minutes to make a list of something a woman or women have said to you.

Choose one and use it to begin your writing prompt.

29

I live in Auburn, California. It's where gold was first discovered in the 1850s and then seekers rushed here to find their riches. The mountains still feel like they hold a lot of richness but a different kind - like the calmness that is felt by going for a hike or the beauty from seeing the moon rise from the mountain tops. Those are moments of true abundance.

Tell about something you discovered that made you feel abundant.

30

For 30 years, my friend (and author) Mark Shaw has reminded me, "You never know when a miracle is just around the corner."

Looking back there were many miracles that happened when I didn't get what I wanted. Two major film deals feel through which made the way for me to end up in Zimbabwe to adopt an abandoned baby named Loveness. Loveness dying and burying her in Zimbabwe made the way for me to focus on healing my body, something I probably would have ignored if I had been successful in Hollywood or had adopted a baby.

There is the miracle of surviving three severe episodes of anaphylactic shock. And there is the miracle of watching my granddaughter come into the world in a circle of women on a dark, rainy night in California.

Tell about a miracle in your life.

31

There is a popular book and show on how to declutter your home. The premise is simple: Don't hold onto something that doesn't spark joy.

I grew up in a crowded house. I was one of five kids and while we each had our own rooms; the spaces of our home were packed with collections. My parents were collectors of antiques. To me, they collected other people's dust. All the bedrooms were on the second level of our house, but my room was on the top floor. Every step and the hall leading up to my room was packed with boxes filled with things my parents were holding onto. I would have to step over and around them to get to my room.

The summer I was eight, my dad gave me the best gift. A large oak tree in our yard snapped in half during a thunderstorm and after dad cleared away the damaged parts, there was just a stump left. The stump was four feet high and Dad spent a Saturday afternoon building a tree house. It was simple, maybe 6' by 6' by 6' with a roof, an open door and two windows. That was my first writing studio.

Describe your childhood bedroom.

Tell how your childhood bedroom reflects or impacts who you are today.

32

Many people pay attention to numbers. What numbers are important to you? How can you write about certain parts of your life using numbers?

In the U.S., we live to an average of 80 years old. That means at age 56, I've already lived 20,000 days and if I die at 80, I have about 9,000 more days left.

Tell about an important day in your life using numbers to recall some of the events.

If you fell in love when you were 20, consider adding the detail of the number: *I'd been alive 7,300 days before I fell in love.*

If you were 35 and nearly died: *The first time I nearly died was on the 12,775th day of my life. It was a Monday.*

Experiment with using numbers in your storytelling.

33

There is an art to storytelling that engages the reader/viewer. Your job is to make the choice of what story you want to tell and find the best way to tell it.

One of the reasons to do the prompts is to move from journal writing and mornings pages and into writing stories with meaning that can be shared with others. Journal writing and morning pages do have value but most often they aren't writing we share with others.

In the *Wizard of Oz*, Dorothy doesn't talk on and on about everything bad that happened to her, instead she follows her curiosity and goes on a journey. Along the way, she reclaims lost parts of herself. The movie is about the journey. The same formula works for our own stories.

Tell about a journey or road trip you've taken.

34

Music is a fantastic way to pull readers into a scene, especially if it's a song most people know.

Choose any favorite song and you will have a prompt for a story to write. Who was I *with* when I first heard Paul McCartney sing the song *Blackbird*? What was I going through as a teenager when The Beach Boys Album *Pet Sounds* was released?

The writing prompt for today begins with:

I don't know if he had a favorite song or ***I don't know if she had a favorite song.***

35

Now we are going to start putting some of the elements together that we've used in our prompts to create a story. With each question, don't think, just write what comes first.

Choose a year of your life:

Now spend a minute answering each of these with two or three items: (If the year you choose is when you are a baby, you will use your imagination to answer.)

What I saw that year

What I heard that year

What I felt (touch) that year

The taste of that year

The smell of that year

Write On.

Pick a song for that year: (if nothing comes up you can always Google the year and choose a song)

The writing prompt begins with the sentence:

This is the moment everything changed...

See if you can work the song and some of the senses from your lists into the story.

36

We love fish out of water stories. (*Big, Back to the Future, Wizard of Oz*) The lead character is put into a world that isn't familiar or comfortable and we stick with them to find out what happens. Many times, along the way, there are characters that show up to guide them. In the end, it's not the outer world that changes for them, it's the inner world.

Take a moment and think of times when you felt like you didn't belong. Maybe spend one minute making a list. Now choose one scene from that list and use that as the beginning of your story.

Tell about a time you felt like you didn't belong.

Who was there when you felt out-of-place?

Maybe use your senses to describe the scenes around you.

37

In many healing circles, you are asked to check-in with your inner child - to listen to them, to hold them, to be with them.

On one of the worst days of my life it wasn't my inner child who showed up for me, it was my elder. It was the voice of a woman who was me, but she was 30 years older than where I was on that day and she whispered to my shattered soul, "You are going to look back on this as one of the best things that ever happened to you."

Move forward in the timeline of your life.

What does your elder self want you to know?

38

I'll never forget the summer I was 13. Queen released "Bohemian Rhapsody" and the song was so different from the easy pop songs I'd been used to singing by K.C. & The Sunshine Band. By the end of "Bohemian Rhapsody" I felt like I'd entered a whole new world. I felt so...so grown up. The summer I was 13 was also the summer my swim coach was diagnosed with cancer.

After it was announced to our swim team that Coach Lee was sick, he never came to the pool again. But I knew where to find him. Coach lived in the house behind my family home so one day when I saw him go out his side door for a walk. I ran towards the front of my house and started on the sidewalk in the direction towards him. I knew we would run into each other.

I saw him first. He was walking extremely slow - so different from the athletic man who had been training me for the past two years. He was the coach of All-Stars and Olympians who were at least five years older than me. I wanted to be my best around him. He recognized my determination when I was 12 and moved me up to practice and compete with older swimmers. I wasn't ready to lose him.

When he saw me, he gave me a weak wave. I'd never been around a sick person before. I didn't know what to say. My steps shortened to meet his pace. His breath was heavy even though our walk was slow.

"Every time you dive into the pool, it's a new race," he said to me. "Anything is possible."

That summer, his cancer got worse, but my swimming got better. I missed Coach at swim meets and practice, but I always remembered his words. That was the summer, I won a race in 100-meter breaststroke against a swimmer who had been to the Olympics. For one moment, I was one of the best in the world for my age group. That summer the music changed and so did I. I learned to believe that anything was possible.

Tell about a time that you lost something/ someone. Include a song as part of your story.

39

Writing memoir or personal history is discovering vulnerable and important parts of ourselves through experiences and people in our lives. In the *Wizard of Oz*, the characters are all searching for something to complete them and someone or something shows up along the way to help them to remember. That's what a daily writing practice does, it helps you to reclaim the unexpressed stories of your heart. Writing helps you remember.

Tell when you found your heart or **Tell when you found your voice (choose one or both).**

40

Have you ever read a book or movie that you love so much you want to start it again?

Tell about an ending in your life that really was a beginning.

41

Tell about the people, moments, places that make life worth living.

42

Tell three things that you are searching for.

43

Where does your love need to go right now?

44

Tell about how the stars, the sun, the moon or a planet has appeared or influenced your life.

45

Tell about a dream.

It's up to you how you interpret the word dream.

46

Tell about your mother or father's hands

or

Tell about your grandmother or grandfather's hands

47

Tell about something you quit.

48

Tell about a moment you or someone in your family spoke up for themselves.

Be specific. Give a scene. Write about how it felt to speak up. Try opening the scene with dialogue.

49

Tell about the last time you tried something new.

50

Tell what you know about the female lineage in your family.

51

Tell what you know about the male lineage in your family.

52

What do you want people to remember about you?

53

When or where are you most at peace?

54

What is something you wish you did less of this past year?

55

What is something you want to do more of next year?

56

Tell about a love story that ended.

57

What voice do you want to hear again?

58

Tell about the last time you cried.

59

Tell about a time you gave permission for someone to touch you.

60

Tell about an early memory of noticing your skin color.

61

Tell about a time someone needed your help.

62

Tell about the last time you asked for support.

63

What do you see when you look in the mirror?

64

Tell about something that is soft.

65

Tell about what happened when you walked out of the door.

66

Tell about a taste that makes you smile

67

Tell about a smell that reminds you of someone you love.

68

Tell about something that shakes.

69

Tell about something you lost.

70

What is something you would like to become better at?

71

What is something you don't understand about life?

72

What is something you love about life?

Write On.

73

Begin the prompt with: *The last time I danced…*

74

What would you do on a gap year?

75

What do you want to do before you die?

76

Notice five things around you right now.

77

Tell about something that is hard to be grateful for.

78

Write a letter from a person who was inspired by you.

79

What place in the world matches how you feel right now?

80

Tell about a moment you slowed down.

81

Tell about an experience that went too fast.

82

Tell a moment in life you want to relive again but with a different ending.

83

Tell how to love (or make love to) you.

84

Tell about a moment that your breath left you or someone you know.

85

Write an apology you never received.

86

What is the life your mother dreamed for you? How is it different from the one you are living?

87

Tell about someone who believed in you when you forgot to believe in yourself.

88

Tell three things that nourish you.

89

Tell about the last sunset.

90

Tell what you know about the language of the heart.

91

Tell about the last time you laughed.

92

Whose laugh do you remember?

93

Tell about a moment you fell in love.

94

Tell a coming-of-age story as a teenager and then again later in life.

95

Tell about a moment that made you a better person.

96

Tell about something that twinkles or sparkles.

97

Tell about a time you stayed silent.

98

Tell about a time you spoke up.

99

Tell an untold story of your heart.

100

Tell about a season that is your favorite (winter, spring, summer, fall).

101

What my body wants to tell you...

102

Tell why you are like the sun or the moon.

Write On.

103

Tell about something you prayed for.

104

Tell what your body feels/felt like on the best day ever.

(And when was the last time you felt really good in your body.)

105

What is in your suitcase?

106

Tell how love is showing up in your life right now.

107

When was the last time you let your body or voice take up space?

108

Write a letter to your body.

109

Tell about a time it started to snow.

110

Tell about a time you forgot to ask for permission/ consent.

111

Tell about someone that you'll never get to know as an older man or woman.

112

Tell about a time you stopped moving.

113

Tell about a smell that reminds you of home.

114

Tell about something new you have learned.

115

What is something you dream of experiencing in this lifetime?

116

Redwood trees lock roots with other trees to create interdependence. Who is part of your support team?

117

Tell about a scar that healed.

118

What is beautiful about you that no one else can see?

119

Tell about an unanswered prayer.

120

When was the last time you played to win?

When was the last time you played for fun?

121

Tell about the things that make you happy.

122

What is something that you released?

123

Tell about a time you didn't tell the whole story.

124

Tell about a time you chose to invest in an experience instead of a thing.

Write On.

125

Tell about the hardest thing you've dealt with in life.

126

Tell about a song that is a soundtrack to this time of your life.

127

Tell about something you gave up.

128

Tell about something you stopped and then started again later.

129

Tell about a home you lived in or a home you left behind.

130

Tell about a stranger who impacted your life.

131

Tell about a time you didn't feel safe.

Write for 15 minutes. If needed, don't forget to shake, dance, or go for a walk after writing.

132

Tell about a time it was too quiet.

133

Tell about a summer job

134

Tell about a time you were lucky.

135

Tell about a memory of your birthday.

136

Tell about starting a fire or tell about the ashes.

137

Tell about the last time you made someone laugh.

138

Tell about running or running away.

139

Tell about an area of your life that needs to be wilder.

140

Tell about a time you lost your joy.

141

Tell what you want to remember about last summer.

142

Tell about the first kiss

143

Tell about a time you said "Yes" when you really wanted to say "No".

144

Tell about something that was stolen from you

145

What is a story you've never shared with anyone?

146

Tell about a language you speak other than English - or - Tell about a time you had to speak a language other than English.

147

Tell about your last gathering with family.

148

Tell about a time you were surprised.

Write On.

149

Tell about a summer memory with family.

150

Tell about a time your voice made a difference.

151

Tell about something good that is happening (or happened).

152

Tell about a landmark in your life.

153

Tell about a time you chose to tell the truth or Tell about a time you chose a dare.

154

Tell about something that has been passed on to you.

155

Tell about a time you smiled and acted like everything was okay, when it wasn't.

156

Tell about the last time you danced.

157

Tell about a person or event that helped resurrect your spirit.

158

Tell about your favorite shoes.

159

Tell about something that makes you feel lucky.

160

Tell about someone you left behind.

161

Tell about something you won.

162

Tell about a place in nature that brings you peace or power.

163

Tell about something a stranger said to you.

164

Tell about a favorite toy when you were a child.

165

Tell about a time someone didn't tell the truth.

166

Tell about a person that changed your life.

167

Tell about a time you got dirty.

168

Tell about a landmark that means something to you.

Write On.

169

Tell about the first time you drove a car.

170

Tell about first day of school.

171

Tell about something you gave to someone.

172

Tell about something someone said to you that you didn't want to hear.

173

What do the color of your eyes remind you of.

174

Tell how you are like your father or mother.

175

Tell about your favorite part of your body.

176

Tell about your favorite song or movie when you were a teenager.

177

Tell what is one of your favorite sounds to hear.

178

Tell about a time you had to take medicine.

179

Tell about the God you believe in.

180

Tell about a birth or death that changed your life.

181

Tell about a time you needed to be silent.

182

Tell about the last time you held someone's hand.

183

Our bodies are 70% water. Tell how your life is like water.

184

Tell about a time you needed to have hope.

185

Tell about a time you drove away.

186

Tell about a time you moved.

187

Tell about a time you protested.

188

Tell about a disappointment or loss.

189

Tell about a betrayal.

190

Tell about the best thing that ever happened to you.

191

Tell about a moment everything changed.

192

Write a letter to your younger self.

193

Tell about a time you didn't trust your gut.

194

Tell about a time you lost faith.

195

Tell about a time you quietly helped someone else.

196

Tell about a mistake you made.

197

Tell about a time you took a risk.

198

Tell about a big accomplishment.

199

Tell about the last time you said, "I love you."

200

Tell about going for a swim.

201

Tell about turning on the lights.

202

Tell about bringing someone to meet your parents (or loved ones).

203

Tell about a moment that mattered.

204

Tell about sleeping next so someone.

205

Tell about climbing a mountain (literally or metaphorically).

206

Tell about getting lost.

207

Tell about your favorite game you played as a child.

208

Tell about something your mother did when you were child.

209

Tell about your first car.

210

Tell about hiding.

211

Tell about a sport you are good at or Tell about a sport you are not good at.

212

Tell about finishing the race.

213

Tell an instrument you play or wished you played.

214

Tell about a person who influenced you.

215

Tell about your first job.

216

Tell about something daring you did.

217

Tell about reaching for her/his hand.

218

Tell about the last time you were nervous.

219

Tell about something you wish you could do better.

220

Tell what you hear when you listen to the voice(s) within.

221

Tell what you wish your mother had said to you.

222

Tell about the first ten years.

or

Tell about the last ten years.

223

Tell about the last time you met someone at the airport.

224

Tell about your first plane trip.

225

Tell about a time you spent too much money.

226

Tell about someone you held as they cried.

227

Tell about a bad haircut.

228

Tell about a good date or a bad date.

229

Tell about the last thing you made for yourself.

230

Tell about your childhood pet.

231

Tell about a friend who always shows up for you.

232

Tell about a favorite sunrise.

233

Tell about a teacher or coach who made a difference in your life.

234

Tell about a time you either swam or floated.

235

Tell about a time you couldn't get warm.

236

Tell about someone who died too soon.

237

Tell about your childhood best friend.

238

Tell about a love story you admire.

239

Tell about something you forgave yourself for.

240

Tell about a vacation that changed your life.

241

Tell about feeling the sand or grass under your feet.

242

Tell about the last time you experienced joy.

Write On.

243

Tell about being underwater.

244

Tell about something you thought to be true, but it wasn't.

245

Tell about an older person who influenced your life.

246

Tell about something a child said to you.

Write On.

247

Tell about something that is/was hard to accept.

278

Tell about a time there was darkness.

279

Tell about something that scares you.

280

Tell about the last thing you bought that you love.

281

Tell about something you threw away.

282

Tell about how your body has changed.

Write On.

283

Tell about the best hug.

284

Tell about someone you need to forgive.

285

Tell about the best day of your life.

286

Tell about the last time you blew out a candle.

Write On.

287

Tell about an area of your life that has healed.

288

Tell about a new friend you've made.

289

Tell about an animal that you'd like to see in this lifetime.

290

Tell about a trip you cancelled.

291

Tell about the last time you dressed up.

292

Tell about the last time you went to a museum.

293

Tell your favorite place to read or write.

294

Tell about the texture of your skin.

295

Tell about how you look like someone in your family (or not).

296

Tell about the place where you were born.

297

Tell about a vacation that ended too soon.

298

Tell about what your body is telling you right now.

299

Tell about an experience that you've never shared before.

300

Tell about something you're good at.

301

Tell about a time you got lost.

302

Tell about the smell of someone you love.

303

Tell about the last kiss.

304

Tell about someone famous who impacted your life.

305

Tell about the bravest person you know.

306

Tell about last day of summer.

Write On.

307

Tell about starting something new.

308

Tell about the worst year of your life or Tell about the best year of your life.

309

Tell about your first home or Tell about your last home.

310

Write the words you need to hear right now.

311

Tell about your favorite team.

312

Tell about a time you didn't get picked.

313

Tell about a time in history you would have enjoyed living in.

314

Tell about being naked.

315

Tell about your superpower.

316

Tell about showing up late.

317

Tell about letting go.

318

Tell about your favorite bird.

319

Tell about the last time you lied.

320

Tell about a song that makes you dance.

321

Tell about a friend who you don't talk to anymore.

322

Tell about the last time it rained.

323

Tell about the first time you saw the ocean.

324

Tell about your favorite holiday.

325

Tell about the last time you felt wise, wild and free.

326

Tell about the last time you did yoga.

327

Tell about a time your vote mattered.

328

Tell about the last time you spoke up for someone.

Write On.

329

Tell about the last time someone said "No" to you.

330

What would feel like a miracle in your life right now?

331

Tell about an idea you had that you never followed through on.

332

Tell about your last birthday.

333

Tell about your favorite numbers.

334

Tell what animal you most relate to.

335

Tell how you've changed in the past year.

336

Tell how love shows up for you.

337

Tell how your education influenced your life choices.

338

Tell the favorite gift you ever received at the holidays.

339

Tell about when it seemed like love slipped away from you.

340

Tell about a time it seemed like angels were guiding you.

341

Tell about something that could have ended better.

342

Tell about a favorite scenic view.

343

Tell about a walk you remember.

344

Tell about a time the lights went out.

345

Tell about a time you were going too fast.

346

Tell about the best parts of your feminine energy and the best parts of your masculine energy.

Write On.

347

Tell about someone important from every decade of your life.

348

Tell about a time you didn't let your body express itself.

349

Tell about a bridge you crossed.

350

Tell about a strange thing that happened to you.

351

Tell how something that happened to you relates to a universal story.

352

Tell a time that you couldn't heal on your own.

353

Tell about something that doesn't belong to you.

354

Tell about something you carried.

355

Tell about something you grew.

356

Tell something you once believed that you don't believe now.

357

Tell about a time you wouldn't let yourself cry.

358

Tell about a time you were a leader or a time you were a follower.

359

Tell about a wish that came true.

360

Tell about what you see when you look into his/her eyes.

Write On.

361

Tell about a promise you didn't keep.

362

Tell about a time it felt like love slipped away.

Write On.

363

Tell about a time you knew you were going in the right direction.

364

Tell about the last time you prayed.

365

Write a letter to someone you forgot to thank.

Ready, Set, Publish

Right on! You completed 365 days of writing prompts. If you are considering writing a book, these are some insider tips and valuable resources. These are things I wish I knew before I published my first book.

Ten Tips on Writing & Publishing

1. Before you write, read Mark Shaw's book, *How to Become a Published Author: Idea to Publication.* It's a good book to read so you understand the business of writing and publishing. Mark gives valuable information on how to write a book proposal and how to find an agent. If you

choose to self-publish, Mark offers guidelines that may save you thousands of dollars. Invest in a consultation with Mark to discuss your book.

2. Start paying attention to the books and genres you like. Beyond the writing, pay attention to how the book is formatted. What do you like about it? What font do you prefer? Will you use quote pages within your chapters? What font do you like for chapter titles? These are all elements a book designer will help create and you can start now by taking notes and photos of designs you like. As a self-published author it's important to make your book look as good as one published by a major publisher.

3. Invest in a few months of Publishers Marketplace, an online forum for agents & publishers. It's $25/month and it will give you an idea of who is buying what genre. Even if you are choosing

to self-publish, this website offers insight into the current trends in publishing. Check Poets & Writers online for weekly updates on agents who want your work. As a writer, it's important to educate yourself about the business of publishing.

4. Invest in a writing retreat. I list some favorites under *Inspire Me*. Writing retreats are good for the soul whether you are writing a book or not. You don't have to consider yourself a writer to go on one, but you may find that you claim yourself as a writer by the time you leave. I offer several writing retreats a year. Writers have joined me in California, France, Bali, Miami and Cape Town. Check my website for info on the next retreats.

5. I chose to self-publish because I knew the genre of the books would be easy to sell (Sensuality & Spirituality). I also took responsibility for

building a platform on social networking (FB and Instagram). Twitter is the preferred platform for writers. Marketing support is one area where traditional publishing is much better than self-publishing; however, if you already have a strong online presence and engage with your followers, self-publishing is a great option. The publishing industry continues to change, and I believe there is always another way to do anything and be successful.

6. Make sure you have an editor for your book. Your book should go through several rounds of copy edits and a final proofreading before publishing.

7. Book covers sell your book! Make sure you invest in a graphic artist who knows book publishing to design your book cover. Your self-published book should look as good as a book published by a major publisher.

8. Join a weekly writers circle. This gives you accountability for your writing and the feedback you receive is extremely valuable. You can Google writing circles in your area or you can create one. You can find details on how to form a writing circle in this book under *Inspire Me*.

9. Look for books in your genre and research who is the publisher and agent. (Many times, you can find the author's agent being thanked in the book.)

10. Write! If you are considering writing a book, the first step is to write. Once you have completed a manuscript - and before you send to anyone to read (especially an editor or agent or Betsy!), make sure to submit your book in the standard format used in publishing. (You can find this info in Mark Shaw's book or Google).

Ready, Set, Publish

Your First Draft is Complete.
Now What?

Send your book to friends for feedback

Instead of asking them to read and review your book, be specific on the feedback you are looking for.

Get a line edit and a manuscript evaluation

A line edit reviews the content and writing style line by line. A manuscript evaluation looks at the entire book. Does the story work and is there a place for it in the current market?

Write On.

Line Edits, Copy Edits & Manuscript Evaluations

Jaime Fleres JaimeFleres.com

Jaime can guide you through every step of the writing and publishing process. She's the author of the book, *Birth Your Story.*

Jennifer Gandin Le

Betsy highly recommends Jennifer. She is wonderful to work with especially for new authors. Jennifer is based in Austin, Texas but works with clients all over the world. JenniferGandin.com

Ann Moller annmoller@gmail.com

Ann Moller has a background in the publishing world. She is an excellent editor and offers coaching sessions for writers. Highly recommended.

Betsy Murphy offers feedback on nonfiction in book length or short stories. She also offers guidance on self-publishing. betsy@betsybmurphy.com

Betsy uses her friend Amanda as a copy editor for many of her books. Amanda is from the U.S., lives in Cambodia and offers her exceptional editing services through the Fiverr website at a reasonable price. https://www.fiverr.com/stylusink

Completed manuscript

Send your book for a final copy edit and proofreading. Complete the copy edit before you send your manuscript to an agent or publisher for consideration.

Ready, Set, Publish

Self–Publishing:
Looking Great vs. Looking Good

Consult an expert for design & formatting of your book. Your book cover is extremely important. Make sure you use a graphic artist who has experience in book design.

A good place to start is to look at books you like to use as reference for book cover and formatting.

Betsy Murphy, Beautiful Infinity Books, offers book consulting from writing through design and publishing.

www.betsybmurphy.com

Write On.

Roz Hopkins and Natalie Winter, excellent for book cover, design & formatting, marketing & publicity materials and publishing consultation.

http://captainhoney.com.au/

From Emily Bohanan is the designer of the beautiful book *Qoya* by Rochelle Schieck

Emily is available for book cover & interior design

Inspire Me

Books to read to support your writing

How to Become a Published Author by Mark Shaw

Bird by Bird by Anne Lamott

The Story of Your Life by Dan Wakefield

On Writing: A Memoir of the Craft by Stephen King

An Old Friend From Far Away by Natalie Goldberg

The War of Art by Steven Pressfield

Big Magic by Elizabeth Gilbert

Wired for Story by Lisa Cron

Inspire Me

Forming a Writers Circle

Here is a suggested format:

Meet for 1 1/2 to 2 hours (depending on how many writers 3-5 is good number).

Everyone brings a story each week to read and get feedback.

Stories should be no longer than 1400 words (and don't have to be complete).

Bring enough copies for everyone so people can write notes on your story as you read. You get all the copies back after you share your story.

You read your story and then one by one everyone around the circle gives feedback: what they liked, what they wanted more of, anything they didn't understand. Rather than it being a discussion, it's feedback only. (This should be 20-30 minutes for each person in group.)

Reading your writing out loud and receiving supportive feedback is a powerful way to commit to writing your book.

Inspire Me

Podcasts to Inspire Creativity and Truth Telling

Notes on Your Notes: A fantastic podcast for creatives
https://www.notesonyournotes.com/

Truth Telling with Elizabeth Dialto: Elizabeth has a diverse range of guests and in addition to being a good interviewer; she's a great listener. I always learn something new.
https://wildsoulmovement.com/podcast/

Write On.

Dear Sugars: With Cheryl Strayed (WILD) and Steve Almond. The final season was in 2018 but the episodes are all available.

https://therumpus.net/sections/dear-sugar/

Radio Gorgeous: A smart, funny, and informative podcast. You feel like you are at a fabulous dinner party with interesting and entertaining conversation.

http://radiogorgeous.com/

Inspire Me

Writing Groups, Retreats & Workshops

Ann Randolph's writing and storytelling workshops and retreats are a favorite. They sell-out so get on Ann's mailing list for info.

https://www.annrandolph.com/

Laura Davis is a pioneer in truth telling, especially around abuse. Twenty years ago, she released a book about sexual abuse. Even in 2014 when I released my first book about healing from sexual assault, people weren't comfortable talking about it. Laura offers writing workshops and retreats around the world. You can also sign up for her email list for

Write On.

free weekly writing prompts - including an online community to post your stories. You can find Laura at https://lauradavis.net/

Betsy Murphy offers both online writing circles and writing retreats around the world.
http://betsybmurphy.com/

Joyce Maynard

http://www.joycemaynard.com

Dani Shapiro

http://danishapiro.com/

Beautiful Writers Group (low monthly fee, loads of resources)
http://thebeautifulwritersgroup.com/

Suzi Banks Baum lovingly guides you to discover the treasure in your stories.
www.suzibanksbaum.com

Printed in Great Britain
by Amazon